NEBRASKA

The Cornhusker State

BY
JOHN HAMILTON

Abdo & Daughters
An imprint of Abdo Publishing | abdopublishing.com

abdopublishing.com

Published by ABDO Publishing, a division of ABDO, PO Box 398166, Minneapolis, Minnesota 55439. Copyright © 2017 by Abdo Consulting Group, Inc. International copyrights reserved in all countries. No part of this book may be reproduced in any form without written permission from the publisher. ABDO & Daughters™ is a trademark and logo of ABDO Publishing.

Printed in the United States of America, North Mankato, Minnesota.
042016
092016

Editor: Sue Hamilton   **Contributing Editor:** Bridget O'Brien
Graphic Design: Sue Hamilton
Cover Art Direction: Candice Keimig   **Cover Photo Selection:** Neil Klinepier
Cover Photo: iStock
Interior Images: Alamy, AP, Ashfall Fossil Beds State Historical Park, Corbis, Dreamstime, George Catlin, Getty, Granger Collection, Gunter Kuchler, Henry Doorly Zoo, History in Full Color-Restoration/Colorization, Independence National Historical Park/C.W. Peale, iStock, Jimmy Emerson, Library of Congress, Lincoln Saltdogs, Mile High Maps, Minden Pictures, National Geographic, National Park Service, Nebraska State Historical Society, Omaha Beef, Omaha Storm Chasers, One Mile Up, Science Source, U.S. Air Force, & University of Nebraska State Museum.

Statistics: *State and City Populations*, U.S. Census Bureau, July 1, 2015/2014 estimates; *Land and Water Area*, U.S. Census Bureau, 2010 Census, MAF/TIGER database; *State Temperature Extremes*, NOAA National Climatic Data Center; *Climatology and Average Annual Precipitation*, NOAA National Climatic Data Center, 1980-2015 statewide averages; *State Highest and Lowest Points*, NOAA National Geodetic Survey.

Websites: To learn more about the United States, visit booklinks.abdopublishing.com. These links are routinely monitored and updated to provide the most current information available.

Cataloging-in-Publication Data

Names: Hamilton, John, 1959- author.
Title: Nebraska / by John Hamilton.
Description: Minneapolis, MN : Abdo Publishing, [2017] | Series: The United
    States of America | Includes index.
Identifiers: LCCN 2015957619 | ISBN 9781680783292 (lib. bdg.) |
    ISBN 9781680774337 (ebook)
Subjects: LCSH: Nebraska--Juvenile literature.
Classification: DDC 978.2--dc23
LC record available at http://lccn.loc.gov/2015957619

CONTENTS

THE CORNHUSKER STATE

I n 1820, United States Army explorer Major Stephen Long journeyed through the Great Plains, including today's Nebraska. The major gazed at the vast, treeless plains and saw a barren land unfit for farming. Major Long called the plains "The Great Desert." He thought the area was a poor place to settle. He couldn't have been more wrong.

Today, thanks to irrigation and hard-working farmers, Nebraska is a fertile land that feeds the nation. The state is beautiful in its own way. Endless rows of corn recede into wide-open spaces. Newly planted trees, their branches waving in the prairie wind, protect the soil from erosion. Ponds and rivers shelter millions of migratory birds in one of nature's most awe-inspiring spectacles.

Nebraska is full of people who love their state and its history. They are also crazy for their university football team, the Cornhuskers, for whom the state is named. Cornhusking is the manual stripping of husks from fresh corn, Nebraska's most important crop.

Each spring, thousands of sandhill cranes stop at Nebraska's Platte River on their annual northerly migration.

At 800 feet (244 m) high, the towering Scotts Bluff is a famous Nebraska landmark.

QUICK FACTS

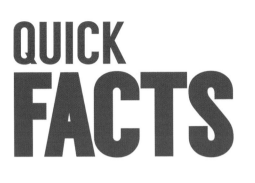

Name: Nebraska is a translation of an Otoe Native American word that means "flat water," referring to the Platte River.

State Capital: Lincoln, population 272,996

Date of Statehood: March 1, 1867 (37th state)

Population: 1,896,190 (37th-most populous state)

Area (Total Land and Water): 77,348 square miles (200,330 sq km), 16th-largest state

Largest City: Omaha, population 446,599

Nickname: The Cornhusker State

Motto: Equality Before the Law

State Bird: Western Meadowlark

State Flower: Goldenrod

State Gemstone: Blue Chalcedony

State Tree: Cottonwood

State Song: "Beautiful Nebraska"

Highest Point: Panorama Point, 5,424 feet (1,653 m)

Lowest Point: Missouri River at Richardson County, 840 feet (256 m)

Average July High Temperature: 88°F (31°C)

Record High Temperature: 118°F (48°C), in Minden on July 24, 1936

Average January Low Temperature: 14°F (-10°C)

Record Low Temperature: -47°F (-44°C), in Oshkosh on December 22, 1989

Average Annual Precipitation: 24 inches (61 cm)

Number of U.S. Senators: 2

Number of U.S. Representatives: 3

U.S. Presidents Born in Nebraska: Gerald Ford, 38th president

U.S. Postal Service Abbreviation: NE

QUICK FACTS

GEOGRAPHY

Nebraska is part of the Great Plains region of the United States. It is also part of the Midwest. It is the 16th-largest state. It is shaped roughly like a rectangle, with a panhandle in the northwest corner. Nebraska is approximately 210 miles (338 km) from north to south, and about 430 miles (692 km) from east to west.

A plain is an area of flat land with scarce trees. In Nebraska, there are some areas with rolling hills, but it is mostly level ground. Much of the state's prairie soil is good for farming, especially the eastern two-thirds. In the semi-arid western third of Nebraska, the land is better suited for raising cattle.

Much of western Nebraska is better suited for raising cattle.

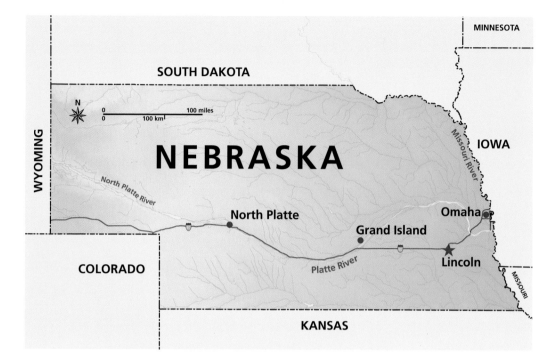

Nebraska's total land and water area is 77,348 square miles (200,330 sq km). It is the 16th-largest state. The state capital is Lincoln.

Nebraska's eastern prairies are fertile because of glaciers that scraped and leveled the land thousands of years ago. When the great ice sheets melted, they left behind rich soil. Windblown soil, called loess, also covered much of the land.

As one travels westward, the land gently rises and becomes more arid. The Sandhills are in north-central Nebraska. It is the largest region of sand dunes in the country. The dunes are mostly covered with grass, which controls erosion and is good for cattle grazing.

Many cattle ranches are in the high plains region of the northwest panhandle. These arid plains are broken in places with steep valleys, rocky badlands, and towering buttes.

The Sandhills of Nebraska
are grass-covered sand dunes.

The Platte River runs from west to east across the state of Nebraska.

The Missouri River makes up Nebraska's eastern border. The Platte River flows 310 miles (499 km) across the state from west to east, eventually emptying into the Missouri River.

One reason many Nebraska farmers are so successful is because of the Ogallala Aquifer. An aquifer is a large underground reservoir of water. It is easy to pump the water out of the ground and use it to irrigate crops. The Ogallala Aquifer is one of the largest in the world. It lies below eight states in the central United States. It is a critical natural resource for Nebraska farmers.

In recent years, scientists have become alarmed that too much water is being pumped out of the aquifer. Conservation efforts are needed because it would take many hundreds of years to refill the aquifer.

GEOGRAPHY

CLIMATE AND
WEATHER

Nebraska can be very hot in the summer, and frigid in the winter. Temperatures can change quickly. When hot and cold air systems collide overhead, extreme weather is spawned, including thunderstorms, hail, or even tornadoes.

The eastern half of Nebraska experiences a humid continental climate. There are big temperature differences between seasons, but there is usually ample rain or snow. The western half of the state is semi-arid. It receives much less precipitation, although it is not dry enough to be called a desert. Statewide, the average annual precipitation is 24 inches (61 cm).

Nebraska's average July high temperature is 88°F (31°C). On some days, the thermometer can reach 100°F (38°C) or more. In winter, cold air is drawn down from Canada, bringing average low temperatures in January of just 14°F (-10°C). High winds blowing across the plains can cause blinding blizzards.

A snowstorm hits Omaha, Nebraska.

Nebraska is within Tornado Alley. Common summer thunderstorms sometimes result in dangerous twisters. On average, 57 tornadoes strike the state each year. Most are weak and whirl only over the countryside, but some form over populated areas and become destructive.

A tornado moves across the countryside near York, Nebraska.

13

PLANTS AND
ANIMALS

When European-Americans first settled in Nebraska, less than three percent of the land was forested. The rest was unspoiled tallgrass and shortgrass prairie. Today, most of that "Sea of Grass" has been turned into farmland for raising crops or cattle. However, there are still large tracts of glassland in the state, especially in the north-central Sandhills and western regions.

Nebraska's prairies are filled with many species of grasses and flowering plants. There are more than 720 species in the Sandhills region alone. Prairie grasses have long roots, which prevent soil erosion. They also provide food and shelter for animals. Some tallgrasses can reach heights of 6 to 8 feet (1.8 to 2.4 m). Their deep roots help them survive the harsh weather conditions on the prairie.

Tallgrass Prairie

Platte Lupine

Prairie Coneflower

Common grasses found in Nebraska prairies include big bluestem, Indiangrass, switchgrass, and Junegrass. Wildflowers splash the landscape with color in spring and early summer. They include platte lupine, prairie coneflower, sunflower, prairie rose, swamp milkweed, western spiderwort, and plains prickly pear. Goldenrod is Nebraska's official state flower.

Sunflowers

Planting trees has long been important to Nebraskans. On the windswept plains of the state, trees give much-needed erosion protection and shade, as well as beauty. Growing in eastern and central Nebraska are cottonwood, ash, oak, walnut, elm, and willow trees. In the western side of the state, it is more common to find pine and cedar trees.

In the early 1800s, large herds of bison grazed on the Nebraska prairies. Scientists estimate there were once 60 million bison (commonly called buffalo) in North America. After decades of overhunting, the herds were almost completely wiped out. Today, thanks to conservation efforts, bison have made a comeback. Some can be seen at Fort Niobrara National Wildlife Refuge in north-central Nebraska.

Other mammals found in Nebraska include white-tailed deer, mule deer, elk, pronghorn, beavers, muskrats, coyotes, prairie dogs, raccoons, jackrabbits, striped skunks, and bobcats.

A female white-tailed deer hides amid the trees in Nebraska.

A sandhill crane leaps up while doing a courtship dance.

Hundreds of species of birds can be spotted flying through Nebraska's prairie skies. The western meadowlark is the official state bird. Common game birds include ducks, geese, quail, and pheasants.

Each spring in central Nebraska, hundreds of thousands of sandhill cranes gather along the Platte River and nearby wetlands. They stop in Nebraska to rest while migrating north to their breeding grounds in Canada and Alaska.

Common fish found swimming in Nebraska's rivers and lakes include bass, crappies, perch, muskellunge, northern pike, trout, and walleye. The official state fish is the channel catfish.

PLANTS AND ANIMALS

HISTORY

Paleo-Indians settled in today's Nebraska about 10,000 years ago, and possibly much earlier. These ancestors of today's Native Americans wandered over the land, gathering roots and berries, and spear-hunting large game such as mammoths and bison.

By the time Europeans began exploring North America, there were several organized Native American tribes living in Nebraska. In the east were the Otoe, Pawnee, Ponca, Missouria, and Omaha tribes. They lived in earthen lodges and grew their own food. In western Nebraska lived nomadic tribes such as the Lakota (Teton Sioux), Cheyenne, Comanche, and Arapaho. They lived in portable teepees and hunted migrating herds of big game such as bison.

Some Native Americans moved from place to place to follow their food sources.

French explorers, including Étienne Veniard de Bourgmont, used canoes to travel up the Missouri River and explore the interior of the New World.

The first European to likely set foot in Nebraska was French explorer Étienne Veniard de Bourgmont. In 1714, he travelled up the Missouri River until he reached the mouth of the Platte River. He named it *Rivière Nebraskier*, which was the Otoe Native American word for "flat water."

About 25 years later, in 1739, French brothers Pierre and Paul Mallet explored Nebraska. They went upstream along the Platte River, traveling westward almost the entire length of today's state.

During the 1700s, both France and Spain claimed the middle of the North American continent. The region changed hands several times. Finally, in 1803, France sold the land to the United States. The sale was called the Louisiana Purchase. (Today's state of Louisiana was just a small part of the area.) The sale almost doubled the land area of the United States. Nebraska was part of the purchase.

President Thomas Jefferson wanted to discover what was in the new territory. In 1804, the Lewis and Clark Expedition travelled by boat up the Missouri River. They explored the far eastern edge of Nebraska. Near today's Omaha, they met with members of the Otoe and Missouria Native American tribes. Soon after the expedition passed through, trappers and traders began exploring more of Nebraska.

Settlers cross the Platte River.

Starting in the 1840s, thousands of settlers, many in wagon trains, followed the Platte River on their journey west to California and Oregon. They were also guided by famous landmarks such as Chimney Rock and Scotts Bluff. Some chose to go no farther and started farms and small communities in Nebraska. The area's population grew. In 1854, Nebraska Territory was formed.

In the mid-1800s, many Native Americans were killed by disease or warfare. Many more were forced to leave their homeland to live on far-away reservations.

Nebraska became a state on March 1, 1867. The city of Lancaster became the state capital. It was renamed Lincoln, in honor of President Abraham Lincoln.

The Sylvester Rawding family were photographed in front of their sod house in Custer County, Nebraska.

Railroads crisscrossed Nebraska by the 1880s. They made it easier to bring much-needed building supplies to communities on the treeless prairies. Before wood was readily available, many farmers made houses out of thick sod cut from the ground. Along with supplies, the railroads brought more settlers to the state.

During the 1880s, Nebraska's population boomed. Ranchers found the land perfect for grazing cattle. The city of Omaha became an important meatpacking center. Farmers were helped by the invention of steel plows to break up the prairie soil, and wind mills to pump water from wells. Sometimes, hail storms and swarms of grasshoppers ruined crops. There were also conflicts between farmers and ranchers over sharing the land. But Nebraska's farmers were determined, even during tough times.

During World War I (1914-1918), thousands of Nebraskans left home to fight in Europe. Nebraska's farmers and cattle ranchers received great prices for their goods during the war. However, when the Great Depression struck in 1929, many people lost their jobs and farmers lost their land.

The state's economy slowly improved during the 1930s. During World War II (1939-1945), the need for food products grew again, greatly boosting Nebraska farmers.

During the second half of the 20th century, advanced machinery and new ways to water crops made farming easier. The size of the average Nebraska farm grew.

Today, Nebraska has attracted new industries such as insurance, health care, and tourism. The state is somewhat less dependent on agriculture, which gives it a steadier economy.

Bomb cases were made and shipped from the Nebraska Ordnance Plant in Omaha, Nebraska, during World War II.

HISTORY

DID YOU KNOW?

• In 1971, paleontologist Dr. Michael Voorhies was walking through gullies in northeastern Nebraska. Heavy rains had exposed some ancient fossil bones in the mud. After digging, Voorhies discovered one of the best fossil beds in the country. It had the bones of ancient camels, horses, deer, turtles, birds, and rhinoceroses. About 12 million years ago, a large volcano in southwestern Idaho erupted, sending a choking plume of ash eastward. The fossil bed marks an ancient watering hole where herds of animals died. Their bodies were covered by the ash and preserved as fossils for millions of years. Today, a museum has been built around the bones. The Ashfall Fossil Beds State Historical Park is located near Royal, Nebraska.

• Carhenge is a replica of England's famous prehistoric Stonehenge monument. Instead of stones, it consists of 39 discarded American automobiles painted gray. It was built in 1987 by Jim Reinders near the town of Alliance, in western Nebraska. The artwork is 95 feet (29 m) in diameter.

• J. Sterling Morton moved to Nebraska Territory in 1854. He and his wife loved nature, and they soon planted many trees and shrubs on their homestead. As a newspaper editor, Morton encouraged people to plant trees to make shade and prevent soil erosion. On April 10, 1872, Nebraska observed the first Arbor Day. More than one million trees were planted. Today, many places around the world celebrate Arbor Day. The date of the holiday varies, depending on the best time of year to plant trees.

• Chimney Rock is a famous rock formation in western Nebraska. Its narrow spire rises almost 300 feet (91 m) above the surrounding prairie. Chimney Rock was an important visual landmark used by pioneers traveling along the Oregon, California, and Mormon Trails. It could be spotted many miles away, which helped guide the pioneers. Today, it is a National Historic Site near the town of Bayard, Nebraska.

DID YOU KNOW?

PEOPLE

Henry Fonda (1905-1982) was one of the greatest Hollywood actors of all time. He starred in dozens of films, portraying soldiers, cowboys, cops, and politicians. But it was his ability to play common, ordinary men that

made Fonda most famous. He won an Academy Award for 1981's *On Golden Pond*, a family drama in which Fonda played a cranky old man who befriends his daughter's stepson at the family's lakeshore cabin. Other favorite movies starring Fonda include *The Grapes of Wrath*, *Mister Roberts*, *Once Upon a Time in the West*, *The Longest Day*, and *The Ox-Bow Incident*. He was also a talented stage actor. Fonda was born and grew up in Grand Island, Nebraska.

Grace Abbott (1878-1939) was a social worker who improved the lives of immigrant children. She was born in Grand Island, Nebraska. After attending college at the University of Nebraska–Lincoln, she became a leading voice in protecting children's rights. As the head of the Children's Bureau at the United States Department of Labor, she fought against the use of child labor in mines and factories. She also worked tirelessly to improve the lives of children in city slums and rural areas. She is a member of the Nebraska Hall of Fame. Her sister, Edith, was also a social worker and educator.

Dr. Susan LaFlesche Picotte (1865-1915) was the nation's first Native American physician. She was born on the Omaha Indian Reservation in eastern Nebraska. Her father was the last recognized chief of his tribe. As a child, she

witnessed the poor health of many of her people and vowed to help them. She earned a medical degree from a school in Pennsylvania, at a time when it was very unusual for women to become doctors. After graduating at the top of her class, she returned to Nebraska to help her people, who were poor and lacked access to medical care. She also served the white community. At night, she often kept a lighted lamp in her home's window to welcome patients.

Warren Buffett (1930-) is a successful businessperson and investor. Born in Omaha, Nebraska, he is often ranked as one of the top-10 richest people in the world. He is the head of an investment company called Berkshire Hathaway. Buffet has given much of his fortune to charity. Despite his wealth (worth at least $61 billion in 2016), he lives in the same modest Omaha house he bought in 1958.

Standing Bear (c. 1834-1908) was a Native American chief. He was a leader of the Ponca tribe. Standing Bear and his people were removed from their land in 1877. They were forced to walk to a Native American reservation in present-day Oklahoma. When he and some of his tribe tried to return, they were arrested. Standing Bear argued in court that Native Americans should have all the rights of other United States citizens. The judge agreed and freed his people.

CITIES

Omaha is the largest city in Nebraska. Its population is 446,599. Together with its surrounding suburbs, the metropolitan area is home to more than 900,000 people. Omaha is named after a Native American tribe that once lived in the area. The city became a hub for trade and industry when railroads came through in the 1800s. Today, Omaha is one of the nation's largest meatpacking centers. The city's economy has diversified and grown greatly in the past few decades. Major employers include banking, insurance, health care, and telecommunications. A major tourist attraction is the Old Market district in downtown, which features restaurants, art galleries, and shops. The city is also home to many blues, jazz, and indie rock bands.

Memorial Stadium

Lincoln is the capital of Nebraska. Named in honor of President Abraham Lincoln, its population is 272,996. It became an important railroad junction starting in the 1870s. Today, the city remains a transportation hub. Major employers include state government, education, and health care. The state capitol building is the second-tallest capitol in the nation (behind Louisiana). The city is home to the University of Nebraska–Lincoln, which enrolls more than 25,000 students. Its sports teams are nicknamed the Cornhuskers. The university's football team is especially popular. The 85,000-seat Memorial Stadium has sold out every game since 1962, an NCAA record.

Grand Island is in central Nebraska, along the shores of the Platte River. In the 1850s, the original settlers thought the area would be a good place for future railroad stations. They built the town near an island named by French fur traders, called *La Grande Island*. Today, Grand Island is Nebraska's fourth-largest city. Its population is 51,236. The city's Stuhr Museum tells the story of pioneer life. It includes a railroad exhibit, a Pawnee Native American earthen lodge, and a log cabin settlement. Nearby, birdwatchers can marvel at the hundreds of thousands of sandhill cranes that roost along the sandbars of the Platte River each spring.

North Platte is in west-central Nebraska. Its population is 24,327. It is located where the North Platte and South Platte Rivers join to form the larger Platte River. The city is a major freight railroad hub. Union Pacific's Bailey Yard is the world's largest railroad classification yard, which is used to separate and sort train cars. On average, more than 14,000 railroad cars pass through Bailey Yard each day. William "Buffalo Bill" Cody once lived on a ranch near North Platte. He named the ranch "Scout's Rest." His house can be toured at the Buffalo Bill Ranch State Historical Park just northwest of the city.

TRANSPORTATION

Nebraska has always been a major transportation hub. During the pioneer days of the 1800s, thousands of people heading west traveled through the state. They often followed the path of the Platte River. When the Transcontinental Railroad was built across the state, it followed the same pathway taken by the pioneers.

Today, Nebraska has 93,770 miles (150,908 km) of public roadways that crisscross the state. Interstate I-80 follows roughly the same east-west path as the Platte River. It is a major roadway used by trucks and passenger vehicles crossing the country.

Union Pacific's Bailey Yard is the world's largest railroad classification yard, which is used to separate and sort train cars.

Railways have long been an important way for Nebraska farmers and ranchers to bring their products to markets in large cities. Today, there are 12 freight railroad companies hauling cargo on 3,375 miles (5,432 km) of track in the state. The most common goods hauled by rail include farm products, coal, chemicals, metal products, and gravel.

Nebraska's busiest airports include Lincoln Airport, Eppley Airfield near Omaha, and Central Nebraska Regional Airport near Grand Island. There are dozens of smaller airports in the state, plus a large military airfield called Offutt Air Force Base. It is in Sarpy County, just south of Omaha.

NATURAL RESOURCES

Nebraska's soil is its most important natural resource. About 96 percent of the state's land is used to raise crops or for grazing livestock. That is about 45.2 million acres (18.3 million ha) of land. The east side of Nebraska has the best fertile soil for growing crops, while the west side of the state has more prairie grasses suitable for cattle ranches. There are approximately 48,700 farms and ranches. The size of the average Nebraska farm operation is 928 acres (376 ha).

Nebraska is called "The Cornhusker State" for good reason. Its most valuable crop by far is corn. It is ranked third in the nation for corn production.

Other important crops include soybeans, hay, wheat, alfalfa, sorghum, potatoes, beans, sunflowers, and oats. Beef cattle, hogs, and sheep are Nebraska's most valuable livestock products.

Corn is harvested at a farm in Bennington, Nebraska.

A pump jack near Kimball, Nebraska, brings oil up from below ground, while wind turbines whirl above ground to create electricity.

Southwestern Nebraska has limited amounts of oil. The majority of the state's electricity comes from coal-fired power plants. Coal is imported by railroad from other states. About 10 percent of Nebraska's electricity is generated from renewable energy sources such as wind turbines and hydroelectric dams. Minerals mined in Nebraska include uranium, limestone, clay, lime, crushed stone, plus sand and gravel.

NATURAL RESOURCES

INDUSTRY

Agriculture is Nebraska's top industry, but fewer than 10 percent of the state's workers are employed on farms or ranches. Automation, large combines, and efficient irrigation methods result in larger farms that require fewer workers.

Many Nebraska manufacturing jobs are related to agriculture. Factories in Lincoln and Omaha produce goods such as farm machinery and irrigation equipment. Nebraska companies also make chemicals, fabricated metal products, plastics, and electronic equipment.

The University of Nebraska–Lincoln opened a new state-of-the-art research park in 2015.

Many of the country's top meatpacking plants are located in Omaha. ConAgra, one of the largest food packaging companies in the United States, has factories and offices in the state.

Omaha is home to many finance and insurance firms, including Mutual of Omaha Insurance Company.

The University of Nebraska–Lincoln employs thousands of people. There are several other major universities scattered throughout the state. Other big public employers include the state and federal governments. Offutt Air Force Base, just south of Omaha, employs nearly 5,000 civilian workers.

Tourism has become an important part of Nebraska's economy. Visitors spend about $4.5 billion each year in the state, supporting more than 44,000 jobs.

INDUSTRY

SPORTS

A Nebraska Cornhuskers fan.

Nebraskans love the football team from the University of Nebraska–Lincoln. During each home game, more than 85,000 fans pack into the university's Memorial Stadium to root for the Nebraska Cornhuskers. The team won its first game in 1890. Since 1970, the Cornhuskers have won five national championships. The university also competes in 21 other men's and women's sports.

Nebraska has no professional major league sports teams. There are, however, several minor league pro teams. Some of the teams include the Lincoln Saltdogs (baseball), the Omaha Storm Chasers (baseball), and the Omaha Beef (indoor football).

A bareback rider at the Buffalo Bill Rodeo in North Platte, Nebraska.

Thanks to the state's many cattle ranches, Western heritage is an important part of Nebraska life. Rodeo is a very popular sport, from high school and college on up to professional. Events include bronc riding, steer wrestling, barrel racing, and bull riding. The Buffalo Bill Rodeo in North Platte is part of the city's Nebraskaland Days summer festival.

Outdoor lovers can find plenty to do in the state, including camping, hunting, hiking, biking, and canoeing. Nebraska has 12 state parks, 68 state wildlife management areas, 6 national wildlife refuges, and 1 national recreation area.

SPORTS

ENTERTAINMENT

Omaha's Henry Doorly Zoo & Aquarium is considered one of the top zoos in the nation. Spread out over 140 acres (57 ha) of land, it houses more than 50,000 animals representing 1,300 species. Its many exhibits include African grasslands, an aviary, and North America's largest indoor tropical rainforest, complete with waterfalls and gibbons swinging through the trees.

The Joslyn Art Museum, in Omaha, has more than 11,000 works of fine art in its permanent collection, including masterpieces depicting the American West. The Sheldon Museum of Art is in Lincoln, on the campus of the University of Nebraska–Lincoln. It has more than 12,000 pieces of artwork, including paintings and sculptures.

Lions

Pygmy Hippos

Desert Dome

People experience life on the Oregon Trail near Scotts Bluff National Monument in western Nebraska.

There are hundreds of museums, theaters, and art festivals throughout Nebraska. Some examples of the state's rich diversity include the Czech Days festival in Wilber, Wild West entertainment at Ogallala's Cowboy Capital, and many Native American pow-wow celebrations held all over Nebraska.

For history lovers, Scotts Bluff National Monument, in western Nebraska, preserves the famous 800-foot (244-m) -tall landmark used by pioneers following the Oregon Trail. Living history performers help visitors experience what life was like for settlers in the 1800s.

ENTERTAINMENT

TIMELINE

8,000 BC—The first Paleo-Indians arrive in today's Nebraska area.

Pre-1800—Several Native American tribes are established in the Nebraska area, including the Otoe, Pawnee, Ponca, Missouria, Omaha, Lakota, Cheyenne, Comanche, and Arapaho people.

1714—Étienne Veniard de Bourgmont is the first European to explore parts of Nebraska.

1803—France sells Nebraska (included in the Louisiana Purchase) to the United States.

1804—Lewis and Clark travel up the Missouri River and explore parts of present-day Nebraska.

1820—The first United States Army military post in Nebraska is established at Fort Atkinson.

1822—First permanent settlement of European-Americans at Bellevue.

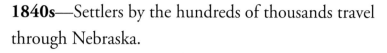

1840s—Settlers by the hundreds of thousands travel through Nebraska.

1854—Nebraska Territory is established.

1867—Nebraska becomes the 37th state on March 1.

1867—Lincoln becomes Nebraska's state capital (replacing Omaha).

1877— Oglala Sioux leader Crazy Horse surrenders, along with 1,100 of his followers, near Fort Robinson, Nebraska.

1948—The United States Air Force Strategic Air Command opens its headquarters at Offutt Air Force Base near Omaha.

2002—Desert Dome, the world's largest indoor desert, opens at Omaha's Henry Doorly Zoo.

2015—Nebraska lawmakers abolish the death penalty in the state.

GLOSSARY

Aquifer

Water that is underground, in the dirt and rock. Unlike an underground river in a cave, an aquifer is water that is saturated in the ground, like a kitchen sponge. Water can be pumped out for irrigation and other uses. Part of the immense Ogallala Aquifer is underneath Nebraska.

Arbor Day

A day set aside for planting trees in the United States and other countries. It usually takes place in April or May.

Erosion

When winds or rains wash away the soil.

Great Plains

The land east of the Rocky Mountains, west of the Mississippi River and stretching from Canada to the Mexican Border. It is mostly covered with grass and few trees.

Louisiana Purchase

A purchase by the United States from France in 1803 of a huge section of land west of the Mississippi River. The United States nearly doubled in size after the purchase. The young country paid about $15 million for more than 828,000 square miles (2.1 million sq km) of land.

Nomadic

People who don't live in one place. Nomads are constantly traveling, usually following animal herds, which they hunt for food.

Oregon Trail

A trail used by settlers and wagon trains beginning in the early 1840s. The trail began in Missouri, went through Nebraska along the Platte River, and then on toward Oregon.

Otoe

The Otoe are a Native American tribe (also spelled Oto) that lived in Nebraska when the first European-Americans arrived. They were one of the first tribes encountered by the Lewis and Clark Expedition (1804-1806) exploring the lands west of the Mississippi River.

Panhandle

An area of land that juts out from the rest of the state. In Nebraska, there is a panhandle in the northwest corner of the state.

Ponca

A Native American tribe that lived in northwestern Nebraska. Chief Standing Bear (c. 1834-1908) became famous for winning a court case against the United States government.

Reservation

Land set aside by the United States federal government for Native Americans.

Tornado Alley

An area of the United States that gets many tornadoes. Nebraska is in this area because cold air from Canada meets warm air from the Gulf of Mexico, causing storms.

Transcontinental Railroad

An American railroad line that stretched from the Atlantic Ocean to the Pacific Ocean, across the continent.

INDEX